Designed by Flowerpot Press
www.FlowerpotPress.com
CHC-0909-0596
ISBN: 978-1-4867-2774-2
Made in China/Fabriqué en Chine

HOW DO SCIENTISTS ASK QUESTIONS?

A BOOK ABOUT THE SCIENTIFIC METHOD

written by
madeline j. hayes

illustrated by
srimalie bassani

THE SCIENTIFIC METHOD

potato
light bulb

dancing
grapes

Science is all about exploration and discovering new ideas and technology. You do not have to be an astronaut or a doctor to use science, although you could be because those are very cool jobs! Anybody can be a scientist by simply learning to think like one.

gummy bear

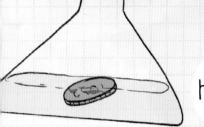

I think I could build a hexagon with marshmallows and toothpicks!

Scientists follow a specific set of steps called the scientific method when they are curious about something. You can use the scientific method to learn new things about the world around you. The best part is you can apply it to whatever you are most interested in! Maybe you want to discover how your dog learns tricks or why clouds form in the sky. Maybe you want to know how to kick your soccer ball really far or how plants grow in your yard. Whatever it is YOU are curious about, try using these steps to learn more. You never know what you'll discover along the way!

Could you please do the dishes?

Maybe I can try an experiment...

OBSERVATION AND QUESTION

How do you know where to start? Do you close your eyes and point to something in your room?

Kind of! You can start anywhere you want with any topic that interests you. Whether you want to learn about food, sports, animals, or video games, you can use science. Observe the world around you and see what catches your eye. Be curious!

It's important to choose something that's interesting to you because that's what's going to motivate you to keep going when the answer isn't clear or easy.

Once you choose a topic, you want to take note of what you know and what you don't know. It is never wrong to not know something. That's the best way to learn new things and figure out exactly what you'd like to know more about.

TAP WATER + GLASS BOTTLE + CAUSTIC SODA + ALUMINUM FOIL + BALLOON → UP

CO_2

A+B

H_2SO_4

$E=mc^2$

Ph

SODA

EUREKa

CURIOUS QUESTIONS

boom

Once you've observed the world around you and chosen a general area of interest, you can start to form your question. Questions are where all great science starts. For a good scientific question, you want to try your best to be specific.

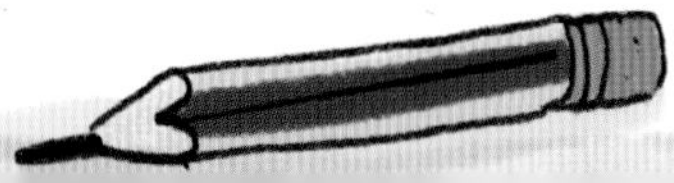

For instance, maybe you want to know whether or not monkeys are cool. Well, yes, they are cool, but that doesn't help us know more about them and is hard to observe in a scientific manner. It's more of an opinion than a fact. Ideally, you want to think of a question you can test. Better questions might be: how do monkeys talk to each other, or can monkeys peel bananas?

H_2O

SCIENCE

Volcano

F_1 F_2 F_3

TOMATO

Now you try! Come up with a topic and a question you're interested in and follow along for the rest of the steps.

BACKGROUND RESEARCH

How do scientists know what and how to research? Are they just born with lots of knowledge?

No way! Scientists don't start off knowing any more than you do. Anyone you admire or look up to had to start at the same place you did as a kid. Scientists know lots of things because they study what other people before them did so they can expand on it.

Charles Darwin (1809–1882)
Naturalist, geologist, and originator of the theory of natural selection

These are some of the greatest scientists of all time!

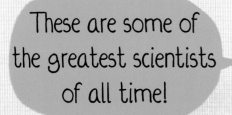

Sir Isaac Newton (1643–1727)
Astronomer best known for his theories about gravity in which he said all objects in the universe have a gravitational force that pulls other objects toward them

$$F = G \frac{m_1 m_2}{r^2}$$

Katherine Johnson (1918–2020)
Mathematician whose studies in orbital mechanics for NASA helped send astronauts to the moon

There are so many more scientists! You might be one of them one day!

Marie Curie (1867–1934)
Physicist and chemist who discovered polonium and radium and pioneered research on radioactivity

Thomas Edison (1847–1931)
Inventor and businessman known for the creation of the incandescent light bulb, phonograph, motion camera, and more

Albert Einstein (1879–1955)
Theoretical physicist who developed the theory of relativity and is regarded as one of the most important physicists of all time

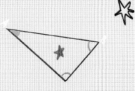

Rosalind Franklin (1920–1958)
Chemist known for her important role in discovering the structure of DNA and for pioneering the use of x-ray diffraction

Percy Lavon Julian (1899–1975)
Research chemist who pioneered the chemical synthesis of medical drugs from plants

It's time to get to work doing your background research. Background research is one of the most important steps because it helps you know what's been done before. That includes what's failed, what's worked, and what more there is to learn.

Here are some of the best ways to begin your background research:

OBSERVE Observing the area you want to study will help you with your background research. For example, if you were wanting to learn more about your little brother, you can learn a lot just by observing the way he acts.

ASK QUESTIONS Talking to people is one of the most effective ways to learn more about what you want to study. Ask your guardian, a teacher, a coach, or even an expert in the subject you are studying what they may know.

READ Check out books from the library or, with permission from a guardian or teacher, search the internet for information. There is so much information out there for you to use!

CHECK YOUR SOURCES!

Some online sources are better than others so knowing what to look for can help! Look at the website URL (websites that end in .gov and .edu are great places to start). Check for an author or confirm the news source. Try confirming the information on another site or offline.

You might find answers to your initial question while doing your background research, and that's okay! Just because someone else has answered your question doesn't mean you shouldn't proceed with your own experiments.

There are three main things you can do if your original question has already been answered: you can test something new, you can test something someone's done before and get the same result, or you can test something someone's done before and get a different result. If you learn something new, that's great! If you get the same result as previous tests, it helps confirm the findings. Science needs to be replicated to be believed. The more often the same result is observed, the less likely that result came from random chance. If you get something different than previous tests, that's important too. You can compare and contrast and try again to figure out what happened to make your results different. No matter what, you are learning something, and that is valuable.

HYPOTHESIS

How do you know what's going to happen? Do you travel to the future to ask your future self?

That would be cool, and maybe one day it will happen if you become a really good scientist. For now, we're left with an educated guess called a hypothesis. A hypothesis is what you think the answer to your question is before you begin testing.

avocado

pineapple

If you did your background research, you should now know more about your topic of interest than you did at the beginning and be able to make some guesses about what might happen.

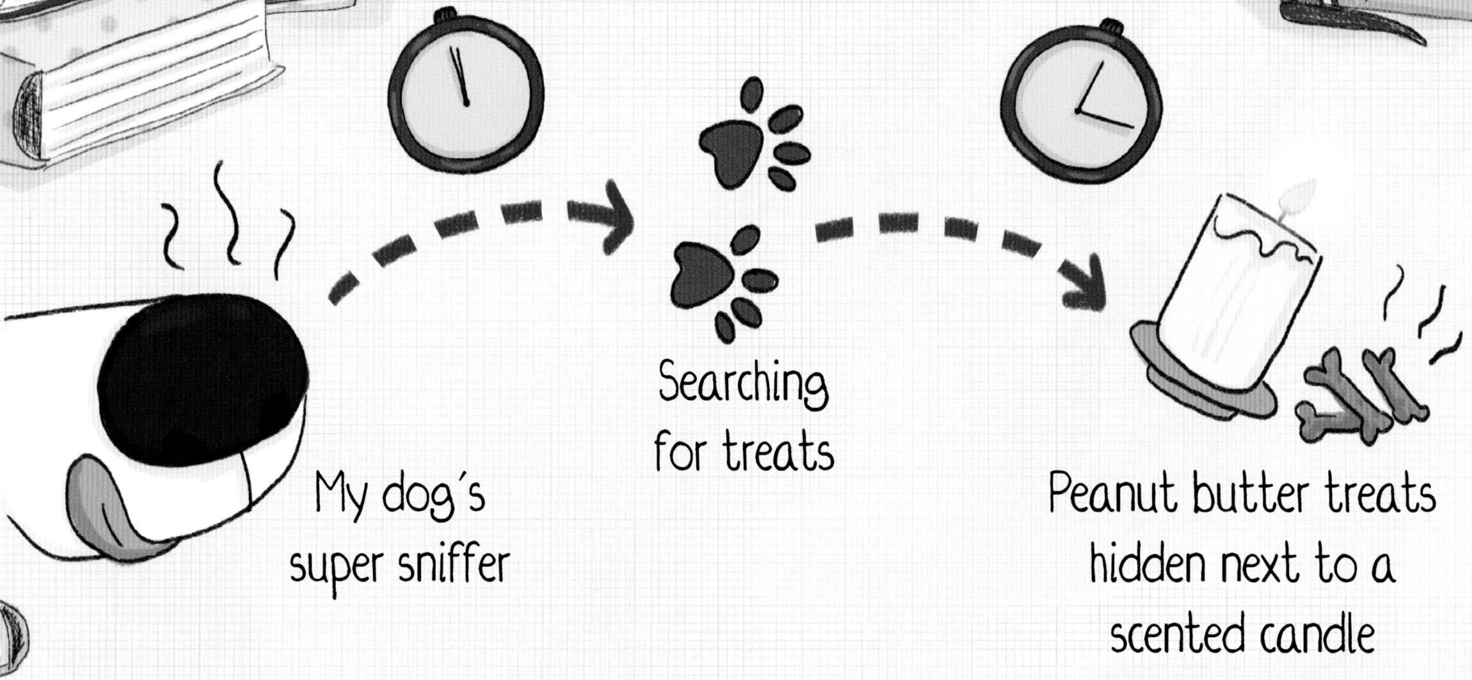

My dog's
super sniffer

Searching
for treats

Peanut butter treats
hidden next to a
scented candle

Now that you're ready to make your hypothesis, try to form it as a conditional statement, also called an if-then statement. A conditional statement is just a way to state your hypothesis in a way that explains if something specific happens, then another specific thing will happen. Not all hypotheses need to be conditional statements, but they are a good place to start.

3, 2, 1!
Go Archie!

if-then

For example, both hypotheses above are looking to study a dog's behavior concerning dog treats. However, there are key reasons why one is better than the other.

1. The bad hypothesis is too general to test well. It doesn't specify a specific dog or type of vegetable, while the good hypothesis specifies "my dog" and "the peanut butter dog treat."

2. The bad hypothesis does not include the if-then statement that helps design a more testable hypothesis. The good hypothesis states that IF the treat is hidden near a scented candle, THEN it will take longer to find. The good hypothesis also gives clear actions: hiding the dog treat then timing how long it takes to find it.

3. The bad hypothesis is not measuring anything specific. It's more of an opinion than something that can be tested. The good hypothesis is looking to test how smell affects a dog finding a treat, which is more specific than if a dog likes or dislikes a treat.

EXPERIMENT

How do you find out if you're right? Do you ask your best friend to find out for you?

No way! This is the fun part! Planning and executing an experiment is what most people imagine when they think of scientists.

Well, here goes test number 4!

When you're ready to test your hypothesis, you first design an experiment that is testable and specific to your question. You want to consider all your background information and previous knowledge about what has worked and not worked before, what resources are available to you, what you might learn from your experiment, and how you can control variables so that you are only testing one thing at a time. (If you test too many things at once, you might get confused about what is really causing things to change and what is a coincidence.)

One thing scientists do to help avoid confusion during their experiment is add controls to their experimental design. Controls are experiment conditions that you add in to show what changes if you do nothing at all. For example, if you wanted to know how well a plant grows in different areas of your house, your experimental condition would be the location of the plant. In this scenario, you could choose four spots as your experimental conditions: a bedroom, a bathroom, the kitchen, and the backyard.

Things such as the soil you use, how often you water the plant, and the type of plant are also variables you would want to control and keep the same across all four conditions. This will allow you to know the differences are probably related to the location and not other factors.

Finally, it is time to gather supplies and proceed with your experiment. This will be specific to whatever you want to test, but no matter what experiment you perform, always be safe, thoughtful, and observant. Scientists commonly write out their plan in a notebook before getting started and then add notes and observations to that plan as they proceed through the experiment. Take pictures, draw diagrams, and record any detail or change you notice. This is all going to help you when you look back at your experiment later. Sometimes the things you think weren't a big deal end up making a huge difference. Be patient and have fun!

Scientists really value peer review, which essentially means getting people around you to listen to your ideas and give you their thoughts on how to make it better. Getting help or advice with your experiment can help you learn more and it might even save you some time and effort if someone points out something you hadn't thought of on your own.

Of course! I'd love to check it out!

Will you take a look at my experiment plan?

BE SURE TO ASK A PARENT OR GUARDIAN PERMISSION BEFORE YOUR EXPERIMENT!

Experiment plan and notes:

Observation notes: _____

What do I see?

Did I water my plant today?

yes   no

DATA, ANALYSIS, AND CONCLUSION

How do you know if your experiment worked? Do you receive an award in the mail for conducting your experiment?

That would be pretty great, but to really know if your experiment worked, you have to look at the data. Data is the result you get from your experiment. Data can be numbers, times, or any other measurement that applies to your experiment.

If you were testing how well plants grow, you would measure their height over time and record those measurements. If you were testing how fast different dogs perform on an obstacle course, you would measure their time from start to finish.

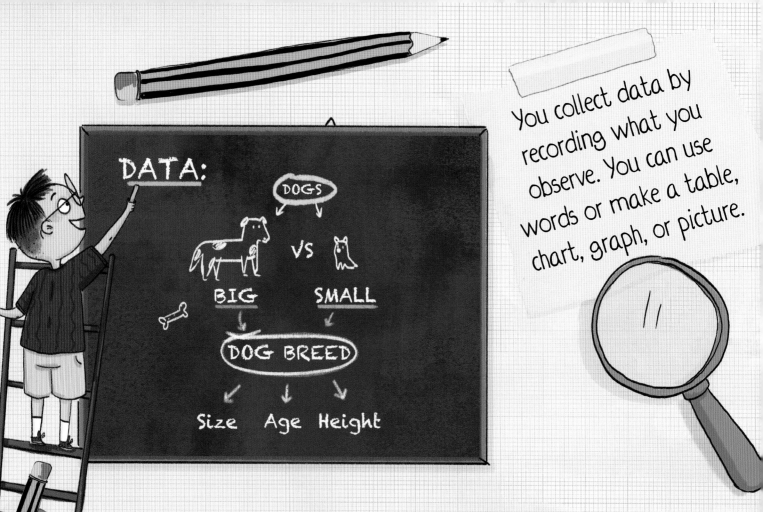

DATA:

DOGS

BIG vs SMALL

DOG BREED

Size Age Height

You collect data by recording what you observe. You can use words or make a table, chart, graph, or picture.

Scientists are all about data. Their goal is to get results they can learn from! Once you have completed your experiment and recorded all your data, you still have to figure out what to do with it.

This is where analysis comes in. When you analyze something, you take a closer look. Take everything you've learned about your experiment up to this point and try to thoughtfully analyze your results.

There are a lot of ways to look at data and interpret results, so it's important to spend time looking at it from different directions. This will help you not be biased toward your own hypothesis and way of thinking.

Once you've analyzed your data, it's time to report your conclusions. You can either reject your hypothesis, meaning you no longer believe you were correct after looking at your data, or you can fail to reject your hypothesis, meaning you still think you are on the right track and your data looks like it supports your hypothesis.

Scientists do not accept their hypothesis as true because they don't know that for sure. There are lots of reasons your data could be supporting your hypothesis, so the best you can do is fail to reject it and follow up with more experiments to increase your confidence in your theory. You might fail to reject your hypothesis that big dogs are faster than small dogs, but you don't know for sure that ALL big dogs are faster than ALL small dogs. This means you cannot completely accept your hypothesis and there is still more to be tested and more to be learned!

conduct experiment

record and analyze data then draw conclusions

experiment supports hypothesis

experiment does not support hypothesis

communicate results

develop new hypothesis and try again

Ask yourself some questions:

Why do you think your data looks the way it does?

Does it surprise you or is it in line with your hypothesis?

Can you perform any analysis or comparisons with your results?

Can you replicate your experiment to gain confidence in your results being true?

REPORT YOUR CONCLUSIONS

How do you know what to do next? Do you look into a crystal ball?

No, you don't need a crystal ball! Once you have drawn the best conclusions you can from your initial experiment, there are two key steps you still have to take.

First, you need to report your conclusions to the world.
You can do this by sharing them with friends, writing a paper
about it, or even gathering a group of peers to discuss your experiment.

The second thing you need to do is help suggest future directions and
experiments. Whether it is for yourself or for others, you want people to
be able to build on all your hard work and learn from it just like you
learned from those who came before you. Take time at the end of your
experiment and analysis to think about what could go differently next
time and what direction the research should take in the future. Even if
you decide you want to move on to researching other topics, suggesting future
directions and questions can help someone else start out in their observations
just like you started at the beginning of this book.

We are here to help!

The scientific method is a cycle, and it is meant to be done over and over again. Each time you should be adjusting the questions and variables slightly so that you learn something new every time you do it. Even experiments that fail to support your initial hypothesis are a learning process, and at any point during the scientific method it is okay to go back to the drawing board and start fresh. You never know what you'll learn along the way!

We'll have the results in a few seconds!

99%

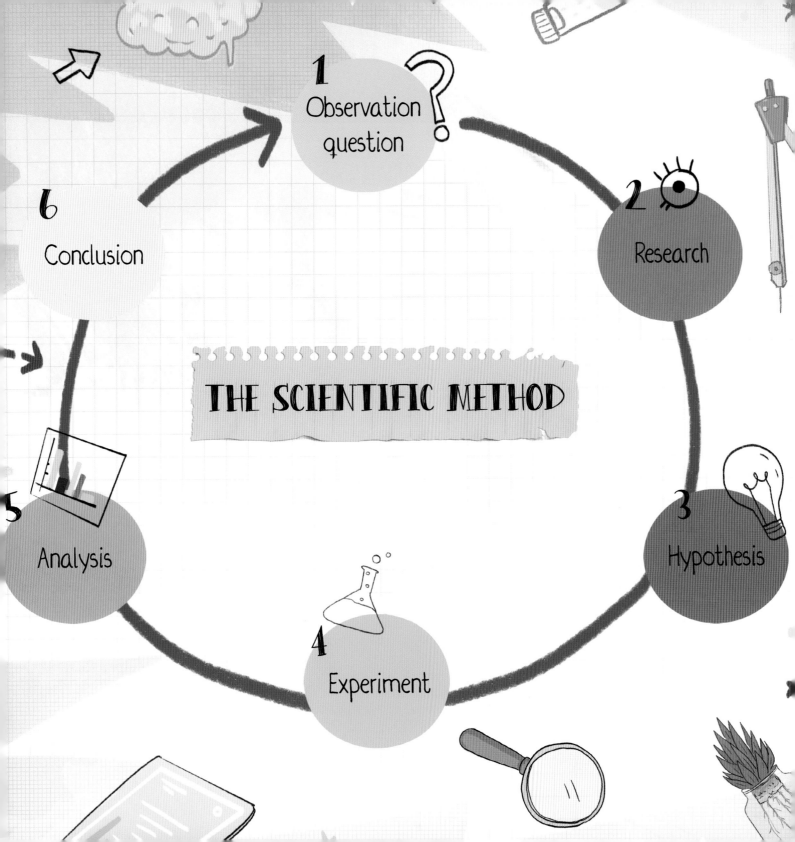

THE SCIENTIFIC METHOD

1 Observation question

2 Research

3 Hypothesis

4 Experiment

5 Analysis

6 Conclusion

SCIENTISTS BEHIND THE SCIENCE

So many scientists throughout history have made discoveries and conducted experiments that have changed the way we see the world or made our lives easier. These scientists paved the way for new scientists to continue making discoveries today. Try some experiments of your own to understand some of the discoveries made by some of these incredible people!

Before you get started, check out some of the real life scientists you learned about in this book!

KATHERINE JOHNSON

THOMAS EDISON

$E = mc^2$

ALBERT EINSTEIN

GALILEO GALILEI

Galileo Galilei was an astronomer, physicist, and engineer who made discoveries about gravity. Other scientists, like Sir Isaac Newton, built theories upon Galileo's experiments and furthered our understanding of gravity. (This is a great example of continuing to do experiments even if someone has made discoveries before you!)

Try it out:
Test Galileo's findings by using some simple items you have at home!

What you need:
- 5" x 7" piece of paper
- Pen

GALILEO'S FINDINGS
Acceleration due to gravity is a fixed value independent of mass. This means that different objects dropped at the same time in the same way should all land at the same time.

Directions:

1. Stand on a chair and hold the pen in one hand and the piece of paper in the other hand out in front of you. Make sure your hands are even. Drop both items at the same time. Note when each item hits the ground.

2. Crumple up the piece of paper into a ball and then repeat step one. Note when each item hits the ground.

SIR ISAAC NEWTON

GALILEO GALILEI

Discussion:
What did you observe when the paper was flat? The flat paper didn't fall as fast because of air resistance. What about when the paper was crumpled up? It had less air resistance and hit the ground at the same time as the pen. All because of gravity!

CHARLES DARWIN

Charles Darwin was a naturalist and biologist who developed theories about natural selection and evolution. His theories came from his research and the discovery of many different fossils while traveling.

Try it out:
Make your own fossils.

What you need:
- 1 cup used coffee grounds
- ½ cup cold coffee
- ½ cup salt
- 1 cup all-purpose flour
- Parchment paper
- Leaves, seashells, small dinosaur or animal toys, etc.

Directions:
1. Mix the coffee grounds, cold coffee, salt, and flour together in a large bowl using your hands.
2. Once the ingredients are mixed, divide the dough into even pieces and roll them into small balls. Place each ball of dough on the parchment paper and flatten each one so there is a smooth space for you to place your item.
3. Make your fossils! Press each item you are going to fossilize lightly onto each dough round. Be careful to lift each item slowly so you don't damage your fossil.
4. Leave to dry overnight.

Discussion:
What kind of fossils did you make? What can you learn about the items from looking at your fossils? What do you think Charles Darwin learned from the fossils he discovered?

ROSALIND FRANKLIN

Rosalind Franklin was a chemist known for the important role she played in discovering the structure of DNA. Her x-ray images of DNA helped scientists learn that DNA consists of two strands, or backbones, twisted in a double helix shape. These strands are made up of nucleotides held together by hydrogen bonds. These nucleotides are adenine (A), thymine (T), cytosine (C), and guanine (G).

Try it out:
Make your very own DNA model using candy.

What you need:
- Small soft candy (you can use marshmallows, gum drops, or gummy candy) in 4 different colors
- 10 toothpicks
- 2 twisted licorice ropes

Directions:
1. Divide the candy into four different bowls by color. You should have about 10 of each color. Assign each color to each nucleotide: A, T, C, and G.
2. On a clean surface, begin assembling your DNA. Carefully put the candy on the toothpicks. Note: C and G bond together and A and T bond together in DNA, so be sure your model is the same. Place the Cs next to Gs and As next to Ts.
3. Once all the toothpicks are full, carefully begin adding the licorice. There should be one rope on the left side of all the toothpicks and one rope on the right side of all the toothpicks.
4. Carefully twist your DNA into a double helix.

Discussion:
Compare your candy DNA to a drawing of DNA. Is it similar?
What did you learn about DNA from this experiment?

GLOSSARY

Analysis – Looking over a set of data to come to an understanding of what it means

Background research – Research that is done before beginning an experiment

Conclusion – The final results found at the end of an experiment

Conditional statement – An if-then statement used to explain how things might happen in an experiment; it is used when stating a hypothesis

Control – A test subject in an experiment that represents a standard item that is not experimented on

Data – The findings gained or known about a subject

Experiment conditions – Things that are tested in an experiment

Experimental design – The way in which an experiment is made, including controls to help provide important data

Future directions – Instructions that are provided for people or yourself to use later when conducting the same experiment again, usually inspired by your findings and any problems from your initial experiment

Hypothesis – What you believe will happen before conducting an experiment (might be different than what actually happens)

Observation – Something you notice about the world around you

Peer review – When someone else looks over a set of data to help confirm the findings

Scientific method – A method of experimentation that includes a question, research, hypothesis, experiment, analysis, and conclusions

Scientist – Someone who studies science in some capacity

Variables – Things that can change between experiments and should be limited during an experiment